NATURAL DISASTERS

VOLCANOES

Luke Thompson

HIGH
interest
books

Children's Press
A Division of Grolier Publishing
New York / London / Hong Kong / Sydney
Danbury, Connecticut

Book Design: MaryJane Wojciechowski
Contributing Editors: Rob Kirkpatrick and Jennifer Ceaser

Photo Credits: Cover, pp. 7, 12, 15, 17, 19, 23, 25 © Index Stock Imagery; pp. 4, 5 © Archivo Iconografico, S.A./Corbis; pp. 8, 9, 20, 21 © Northwind; p. 26 © Gary Braasch/Corbis; pp. 28, 29 © Associated Press AP/AP Wide World Photos; pp. 31, 33 © Roger Ressmeyer/Corbis; p. 35 © Joel W. Rogers/Corbis; p. 36 © Michael T. Sedam/Corbis; p. 39 © Ron Sanford/International Stock

Visit Children's Press on the Internet at:
http://publishing.grolier.com

Library of Congress Cataloging-in-Publication Data

Thompson, Luke.
    Volcanoes / by Luke Thompson.
      p. cm. – (Natural disasters)
    Includes bibliographical references and index.
    ISBN 0-516-23367-X (lib. bdg.) – ISBN 0-516-23567-2 (pbk.)
    1. Volcanoes—Juvenile literature. [1. Volcanoes.] I. Title.

QE521.3.T48 2000
551.21—dc21
                                                00-026959

CONTENTS

INTRODUCTION

The most famous volcano eruption of all time happened long ago in an area that is now Italy. Two cities, Pompeii and Herculaneum, lay at the foot of Mount Vesuvius. On August 24, in 79 A.D., Mount Vesuvius blew its top. First, it sent a huge, black cloud of ash and rock shooting into the air. The cloud shot out of the volcano with so much force that it went 12 miles (19 km) high and turned the sky black. Eventually, all this ash and rock fell to the earth. When it did, it buried the entire city of Pompeii and all of its citizens.

Next, Vesuvius spewed waves of hot, liquid rock, called lava. A fiery flood poured down on Herculaneum. People tried running toward the Bay of Naples, but they could not outrun this river of fire. More than 20 feet (6 m) of volcanic rock smothered the city.

Mount Vesuvius shot deadly fire, rock, and ash during its famous eruption in 79 A.D.

A volcano is an opening in Earth's surface. Volcanoes let out hot, liquid rock from inside Earth. They also may let out ash, solid rock, and gases. When this hot matter pours or shoots out of a volcano, it is called an eruption.

Most volcanoes are mountains. These mountains form when hot, liquid rock called lava cools around the volcano's opening. With each eruption, layers of hardened lava build up. As more eruptions occur over time, a volcano can grow bigger and bigger.

Some of the most beautiful mountains on Earth have been created by volcanic eruptions. But volcanic eruptions throughout history also have been very deadly. People who live near volcanoes hope that they never see an eruption.

Hot, liquid rock pours out of an erupting volcano.

CHAPTER ONE

HOW A VOLCANO FORMS

In August 1883, a volcano on the Indonesian island of Krakatoa erupted in a huge explosion. Two-thirds of the 7-mile-long (11-km-long) island was destroyed instantly. A column of ash and smoke blew 16 miles (26 km) into the sky. Red-hot ash fell and covered the rest of the island. In some places the ash was 65 yards (60 m) deep. The eruption was so powerful that it sent 115-foot (35-m) waves toward the islands of Java and Sumatra. Nearly 36,500 people drowned in these giant waves.

The eruption is believed to have been the loudest sound ever made on Earth. It sounded as loud as a cannon blast to people 2,790 miles (4,500 km) away. Scientists think that the force of the explosion was ten thousand times greater than the atomic bomb that was dropped on Hiroshima, Japan.

This woodcut shows what Krakatoa looked like—before the 1883 eruption that destroyed two-thirds of the island.

Volcanoes form deep in Earth. Earth is made up of three layers: the crust, the mantle, and the core. The crust is the top layer. Its thickness varies. It can be from 4 to 43 miles (6 to 69 km) thick. The crust is broken into large pieces of rock, called plates. Plates move very slowly over Earth's middle layer, called the mantle. The mantle is nearly 80 percent of Earth's size. It is about 1,800 miles (2,898 km) thick. The mantle surrounds Earth's center, or core.

Temperatures are extremely hot close to the core. Core temperatures reach 6,700° F (3,704° C). At such temperatures, rock melts. It turns into molten (liquid-hot) rock. This molten rock is called magma. The mantle is made up of solid rock, but it has pockets of magma, too.

Scientists believe that magma from the mantle causes Earth's plates to move. Magma rises toward the crust and cools. Then, it sinks

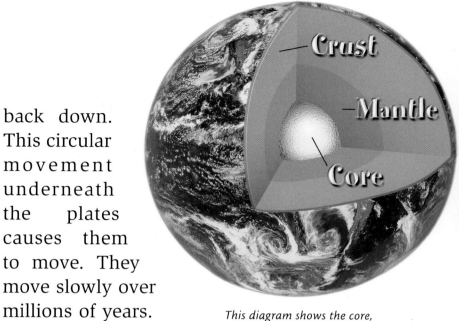

back down. This circular movement underneath the plates causes them to move. They move slowly over millions of years.

This diagram shows the core, mantle, and crust of Earth.

As the plates move, they rub against each other. Magma pushes up through places in the crust where plates meet. Magma can come from as shallow as 1 mile (1.61 km) or as deep as 100 miles (161 km) underground. Magma escapes through an opening in Earth's surface. These places are called volcanoes. Many volcanoes form where plates meet. Sometimes, though, magma melts through the middle of a plate. This kind of melting point is called a hot spot.

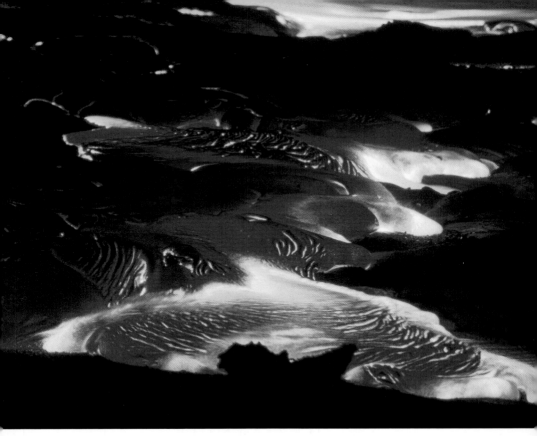

Lava can flow at speeds of more than 80 miles (129 km) per hour.

GAS

As rock turns into magma, it gives off hot gas. This gas is made up of steam and chemical compounds. The most common volcanic gases are carbon dioxide, water vapor, sulfur dioxide, and hydrogen sulfide. Gases rise when they get hot. The underground gas pushes its way out of the mantle through underground passages. These passages lead up to Earth's crust and out the opening of the volcano. This opening is called a vent. As the hot gas pushes upward, it pushes magma up with it. Once in the crust, the gas and magma collect below the surface in pockets. These pockets are called magma chambers. Sometimes, the pressure in these chambers can become too great. Then it forces the magma out through fissures (cracks in the Earth).

LAVA

Magma that escapes onto Earth's surface is called lava. Sometimes, lava is thin and runny. Other times, it is thick and gooey. Lava flows downhill from volcano vents. Lava flows have been known to travel at speeds of more than 80 miles (129 km) per hour. Some lava flows cover more than 100 square miles (161 sq. km) of land.

VOLCANIC ASH AND DUST

Volcano eruptions often send many tiny pieces of dust and ash into the air. Volcanic dust particles are less than .01 inch (.25 mm) in diameter. Volcanic dust is so fine that it stays in the air for a long time. Ashes from eruptions are burnt splinters less than .2 inch (.5 cm) in diameter. Ash shoots out and then falls to the ground. Then it mixes with lava and mud.

VOLCANO TYPES

There are two types of volcanoes: fissure volcanoes and central volcanoes. The shape of a volcano and the way that a volcano erupts determine its type.

Fissure Volcanoes

Fissure volcanoes form when lava comes out of long fissures in the crust. These fissures can be many miles long. Because these fissures are so long, lava oozes out and spreads over the

When lava cools, it forms volcanic rock.

area. When the lava cools, it forms a plain of volcanic rock.

Central Volcanoes

Central volcanoes form when lava comes out of one large, central vent. When the lava cools, it forms a cone of volcanic rock around the vent. Each time the volcano erupts, more lava cools around the volcano. These eruptions cause the volcano to grow larger over time.

There are many different types of central volcanoes. These types include cinder cones, composites, domes, and shields.

- **Cinder Cones** Cinder cones look like low, wide mountains with their tops sliced off. Cinder cones form when large amounts of ash and cinders (burning ashes) erupt out of the vent. The Paricutín volcano in Mexico is a famous cinder cone volcano. It formed during nearly continuous eruptions from 1943 to 1952.
- **Composites** Composite volcanoes are very tall mountains that rise from a wide base to a small, round vent. Composite volcanoes rise as high as 8,000 feet (2,426 m) above the ground. Composites form when smaller openings form around the main vent. Composite volcanoes can be very beautiful from a distance. Some of the world's most famous volcanoes are composite volcanoes.

Mount St. Helens in the state of Washington is a composite volcano.

Mount Fuji in Japan, Mount Etna in Italy, and Mount St. Helens in the United States are all composite volcanoes.

• **Domes** Dome volcanoes are very steep and rounded. They form when thick lava pours out of the vent and cools very fast. The eruption of Mount Hood in Oregon two hundred years ago formed a dome volcano.

• **Shields** Shield volcanoes are low, dome-shaped volcanoes that spread over a large area. When lava oozes slowly out of a vent, it cools and hardens into a broad cone. Some of the largest volcanoes are shield volcanoes, including the world's largest volcano, Mauna Loa in Hawaii.

CALDERAS

Some huge eruptions can spew out hundreds of cubic miles of lava. Such a giant eruption leaves an empty pocket underneath the volcano. After the eruption, the volcano collapses into the empty space beneath it. This creates a huge depression in the land, called a caldera. Some calderas can be 15 miles (24 km) wide and several miles deep. Often, rainwater can collect in a caldera and form a lake. Crater Lake in southwestern Oregon is a famous example of a caldera lake.

DID YOU KNOW?

The word volcano comes from Vulcan, the Roman god of fire. The Romans believed that Vulcan lived underneath an island volcano.

Some volcanic eruptions form craters, called calderas, such as this one in Hawaii.

CHAPTER TWO

ERUPTIONS

Mount Pelée stood above the Caribbean island of Martinique for hundreds of years without erupting. Then, in May 1902, it began to give warning signals. For nearly a week, Mount Pelée sent ash into the air. The sky above the island turned dark during the daytime. The streets of the nearby city of St. Pierre were covered with ash. Also, minor earthquakes shook the island of Martinique. Even so, the people of St. Pierre felt that they had nothing to worry about. They were very wrong.

Mount Pelée erupted on the morning of May 8, 1902. It exploded with full force and sent a huge cloud of volcanic material rocketing into the air. A second burst followed. Lava flowed down the sides of the mountain, toward St. Pierre, at the speed of 100 miles (161 km) per hour. In just minutes, thirty thousand people were buried underneath burning rock and ash.

Mount Pelée erupted in 1902, killing thirty thousand people in Martinique.

There are six different types of volcanic eruptions. These types are based on the strength of the eruption. From weakest to strongest, they are: Icelandic, Hawaiian, Strombolian, Vulcanian, Peléan, and Plinian.

ICELANDIC AND HAWAIIAN

Icelandic and Hawaiian eruptions are minor eruptions. During both, lava oozes slowly from fissures. Icelandic eruptions happen in fissure volcanoes. Hawaiian eruptions happen in central volcanoes. Lava from Hawaiian eruptions flows down mountainsides as hot fudge does over ice cream. Both types are named after places where they are common. However, Icelandic and Hawaiian eruptions can happen throughout the world.

STROMBOLIAN AND VULCANIAN

During Strombolian and Vulcanian eruptions, thick lava blocks the vent and keeps hot gases

Strombolian eruptions send out hot clouds of gas, lava, and rock.

from escaping. Pressure builds up until gas, lava, and solid rock shoot out of the vent. Vulcanian eruptions are stronger than are Strombolians and often produce dark clouds of ash and rock. These two types of eruptions are named after Stromboli and Vulcano, two volcanic islands in Italy.

PELÉAN AND PLINIAN

Peléan eruptions spew thick mixtures of lava, rock, and gas into the air. Peléans are so strong that they often blow up part of the mountain. Plinian eruptions are the strongest type of eruptions. During a Plinian eruption, the center of the volcano explodes. A mushroom-shaped cloud rises from the volcano. This cloud can hang over an area for several hours. The eruption of Vesuvius in 79 A.D. was a Plinian blast.

RIVERS OF FIRE

Explosive eruptions, especially Vulcanian and Peléan blasts, throw chunks of earth into the sky. Large eruptions produce rivers of fiery rock. These volcanic floods are called pyroclastic flows. Pyroclastic flows as hot as 1,470° F (800° C) can pour downhill at speeds of 200 miles (322 km) per hour. Unlucky victims are likely to be burned or even crushed by pyroclastic flows.

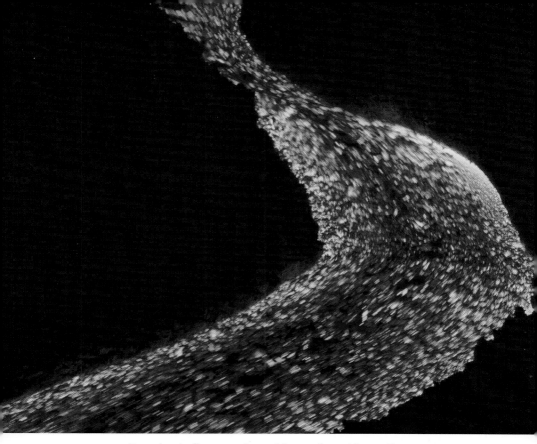

*Pyroclastic flows, such as this one from Mount Etna,
can reach speeds of 200 miles (322 km) per hour.*

Pyroclastic flows are made up of heavy rock. They can only flow downhill from the volcano. Sometimes, though, pyroclastic material mixes with a lot of hot gas. If enough gas mixes with the pyroclastic rock, the gas-rock mixture actually can travel uphill. This combination of rock and gas is called a pyroclastic surge.

Large volcanic eruptions send clouds of deadly ash and gas high into the atmosphere.

AIRBORNE ASH

Lava and deadly temperatures are not the only dangers associated with volcanic eruptions. Volcanic ash can travel for hundreds of miles from the actual eruption site. As it spreads through the atmosphere, this ash makes it difficult (or impossible) to see or breathe. It pollutes drinking water and kills plants. If ash is thick and heavy enough, it can cause roofs of structures to collapse. Clouds of ash can clog jet and car engines, making it very difficult for officials to search an area for survivors.

DEADLY GAS CLOUDS

Eruptions release huge clouds of gas. Sometimes, this gas can make people suffocate (run out of air). These gas clouds can even be poisonous. Volcanic activity can produce deadly gases such as hydrogen sulfide, carbon monoxide, carbon dioxide, and sulfur dioxide. In August 1986, a caldera in Cameroon, West Africa, released a cloud of carbon dioxide that killed 1,700 people.

DID YOU KNOW?

Many more volcanoes exist underwater than exist on land. The most active volcanoes in the world are in the middle of the Atlantic Ocean. They are gathered in an area called the Mid-Atlantic Rift Zone.

CHAPTER THREE

PREDICTION AND SAFETY

In the late 1970s, two scientists studied volcanic rock around Mount St. Helens in Washington state. Mount St. Helens is a volcano that had last erupted in 1857. In 1978, the scientists released a report that said the volcano could erupt before the end of the century. Officials warned local residents to leave the area. Mount St. Helens was closed off to the public.

Scientists continued to study the volcano. On the morning of May 18, 1980, David Johnston was collecting data on Mount St. Helens from an observation post 6 miles (9.7 km) away. Unfortunately, he did not know what lurked inside the mountain.

Just after 8:30 A.M., Mount St. Helens exploded in a huge Plinian eruption. Volcanic matter shot 15 miles (25 km) into the sky in less than thirty minutes. The explosion spewed

Luckily, local residents were warned before Mount St. Helens erupted in May 1980.

out 20-foot (6-m) boulders. Rivers of mud and volcanic rock 50 feet (15 m) deep poured down the mountain at speeds of 90 miles (145 km) per hour. The mountain caved in, forming a giant crater. Johnston, along with fifty-seven others, died in the eruption.

Scientists who study volcanoes are called volcanologists. When scientists study a volcano, one of the first things they want to figure out is whether the volcano can or will erupt.

Scientists have four different categories in which to classify volcanic activity. They are active, intermittent, dormant, and extinct.

ACTIVE VOLCANO

A volcano that constantly erupts over long periods of time is called an active volcano. Stromboli is a volcanic island near Italy that has been erupting on a regular basis for

The volcanic island of Stromboli erupts about every twenty minutes.

several years. This volcano is known as "the lighthouse of the Mediterranean Sea" because it is always glowing. Stromboli erupts nearly every twenty minutes.

INTERMITTENT VOLCANO

An intermittent volcano erupts much less often than does an active volcano. Its eruptions usually occur off and on at regular times. Each eruption is followed by a "down time" in which the volcano is not erupting. A down time may last anywhere from a few months to one hundred years.

DORMANT VOLCANO

A dormant volcano is a volcano that is not active but has the possibility to become active again. Dormant volcanoes also are called sleeping volcanoes. Lassen Peak in California and Mount Rainier in Washington are dormant volcanoes.

EXTINCT VOLCANO

An extinct volcano is one that has not been active for thousands of years. There are hundreds of extinct volcanoes all over the world. Scientists are confident that these volcanoes will never erupt again.

MEASURING ERUPTIONS

Some volcanologists have created the Volcanic Explosivity Index (VEI) to measure the size of eruptions. VEI measurements are based on different factors. These factors include the amount of ash and lava ejected from the volcano, and how big an area it covers. The VEI is a scale of 0 to 8. A rating of 8 is the most explosive eruption. The Mount St. Helens eruption in 1980 had a VEI rating of 5. Volcanologists believe that the 1883 Krakatoa explosion had a VEI rating of 6. The 1815 eruption in Tambora, Indonesia, is believed to be the most explosive eruption ever recorded. Volcanologists have estimated that it was a 7 on the VEI and that it ejected as much as 80 times more ash than did the 1980 Mount St. Helens eruption.

One thing that the VEI does not measure is an eruption's effect on people. Even a small volcanic

A volcanologist measures the strength of a volcano's eruption.

eruption can be deadly if it happens near a town or city. For example, scientists estimated that a 1792 eruption in Japan had a VEI of 2. However, that eruption either killed or injured fifteen thousand people.

VOLCANOES IN AMERICA

There are only six hundred active volcanoes on Earth. As many as sixty-eight are in the United States. Only Japan and Indonesia have more active volcanoes than does the United States. Most U.S. volcanoes are located in remote areas of Alaska and Hawaii. However, twenty volcanoes can be found in the continental United States. Almost all of these are close to populated areas.

Mount Rainier, Washington

Mount Rainier is a 14,411-foot (4,392-m), active volcano that looms above the city of Seattle, Washington. Mount Rainier is one of several

Mount Rainier looms on the horizon near the city of Seattle.

volcanoes in the Cascade mountain range. This range is one of the most active volcano areas in the world. Seven volcanoes have erupted in the Cascades in the past two hundred years. Many more will most likely erupt in the near future. Scientists say Mount Rainier is definitely one of them. It last erupted in 1882. Its next eruption could come in five hundred years—or in five years. Some people say living in Seattle is like living in the shadow of a monster. Others don't think twice about the volcano. About ten thousand people climb Mount Rainier every year.

Kilauea and Mauna Loa, Hawaii

The Hawaii Volcanoes National Park has some of the world's most frightening volcanoes. Kilauea is 50 miles (80 km) long and 14 miles (23 km) wide. It has had a series of small eruptions since 1983. Kilauea lies to the southeast of an even bigger volcano, Mauna Loa. Mauna Loa is 70 miles (113 km) long and

30,000 feet (91 m) high. It is the largest volcano on the planet. It last erupted in 1984, when its lava flow reached to within 4 miles (6.5 km) of the city of Hilo.

Mount Hood

At 11,237 feet (3,425 m), Mount Hood is the tallest mountain in Oregon. It is popular with skiers, hikers, and rock climbers. It's also a volcano that began forming about 500,000 years ago. Its last series of eruptions occurred between 180 and 250 years ago.

VOLCANO PREDICTION

Most volcano eruptions cannot be predicted. However, volcanoes may give warning signs before they erupt. Sometimes a volcano will grow slightly larger before it erupts. It grows because of the magma that collects underneath it. The temperature around the volcano may increase. Steam may pour from its vent.

Mount Kilauea in Hawaii is one of the largest volcanoes on Earth.

Volcanologists use different tools to predict eruptions. They use an instrument called a tilt-meter to measure the size of a volcano. They use a thermometer to check for increases in temperature. Gas detectors are used to check for volcanic gas. Scientists also use seismographs to measure vibrations underneath volcano areas. The ground beneath a volcano is very unstable. Earthquakes often happen along with eruptions. If a seismograph picks up vibrations underneath a volcano, it may be a sign that an eruption will happen soon.

VOLCANO SAFETY

Millions of Americans live in areas that could be affected by eruptions. If you are one of these people, you should remember these safety tips:

• If a volcano erupts near your home, get away as far and as fast as you can.

• Trying to find a safe place to hide during an eruption is risky. Flowing lava can destroy

Officials closed this road in the Hawaii Volcanoes National Park due to a dangerous lava flow.

everything in its path, even the strongest buildings. Dust and ash sometimes fall in such large amounts that buildings collapse under the weight.

• If officials issue a volcano warning, always take it seriously. Many volcano-related deaths happen because people think a volcano warning is a false alarm.

Fact Sheet ·······

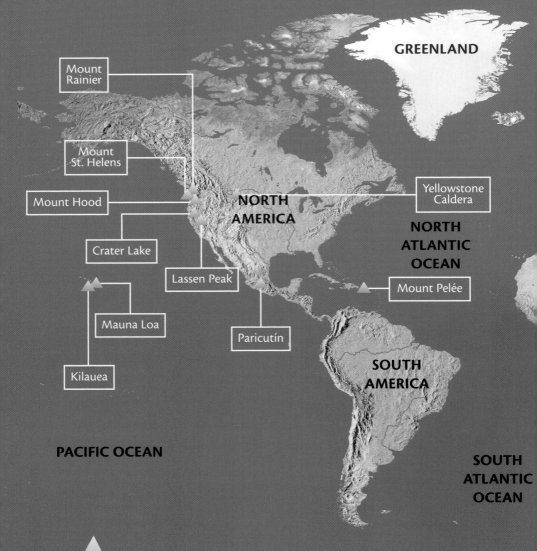

GREENLAND

Mount Rainier

Mount St. Helens

Mount Hood

Crater Lake

Lassen Peak

Mauna Loa

Kilauea

Paricutín

NORTH AMERICA

Yellowstone Caldera

NORTH ATLANTIC OCEAN

Mount Pelée

SOUTH AMERICA

PACIFIC OCEAN

SOUTH ATLANTIC OCEAN

The triangles show the locations of volcanoes mentioned in this book.

Volcano Locations

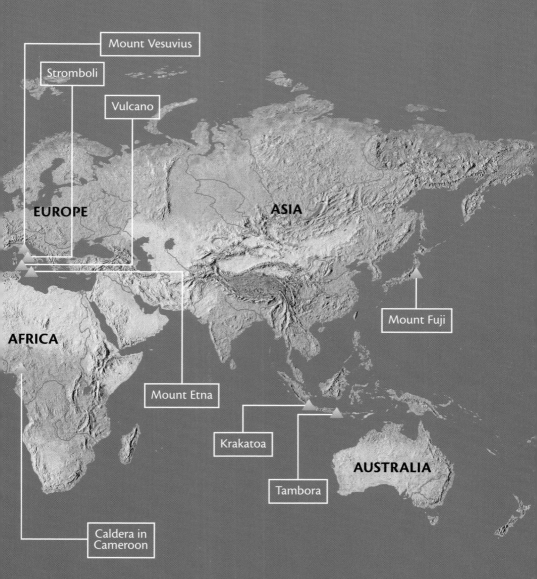

Mount Vesuvius

Stromboli

Vulcano

EUROPE

ASIA

Mount Fuji

AFRICA

Mount Etna

Krakatoa

AUSTRALIA

Tambora

Caldera in Cameroon

NEW WORDS

active volcano a volcano that erupts continuously over long periods of time

caldera a huge depression at the top of a collapsed volcano

central volcano a tall volcano that forms around one central opening

cinder cone volcano a wide, low volcano with a flat top

composite volcano a very tall volcano that rises from a wide base to a narrow top; they are formed by more than one opening

core the center of Earth

crust the top layer of Earth

dome volcano a steep, rounded volcano formed by thick, fast-cooling lava

dormant when a volcano has not erupted for a long time

erupt when lava, rocks, and ash pour out of a volcano

extinct when a volcano will not erupt again

fissure volcano a volcano in which lava oozes out of a long fissure

fissures cracks in Earth

Hawaiian eruption a minor eruption during which lava flows out of a central volcano

hot spot an area where magma seeps through the crust and volcanoes are formed

Icelandic eruption the smallest type of eruption, during which lava oozes out of long cracks in Earth

intermittent when a volcano erupts off and on

lava melted rock after it flows or shoots out of a volcano; aboveground magma

lava flow the movement of hot lava over the surface of Earth

magma hot melted rock below Earth's surface; it turns into lava when it moves above ground

magma chamber a large section beneath the crust where magma collects

mantle the middle layer of Earth

molten melted, or liquid-hot

Peléan eruption a major eruption during which a mountaintop breaks off in an explosion of lava, rocks, and gas

plates huge sections of rock that make up Earth's crust

NEW WORDS

Plinian eruption the largest type of volcano eruption

pyroclastic flow a flood of volcanic rock

pyroclastic surge a rising mixture of volcanic rock and gas

seismograph a tool that measures vibrations in Earth's crust

shield volcano a low, wide, domed-shape volcano

Strombolian eruption an eruption in which gas, lava, and rock shoots out of the volcano opening

suffocate to run out of air

tiltmeter a tool that measures the size of a volcano

vent an opening in a volcano through which magma escapes

Volcanic Explosivity Index (VEI) a scale used to grade volcanic eruptions

volcanologist a scientist who studies volcanoes

Vulcanian eruption an eruption during which dark clouds of ash and rock shoot into the air

FOR FURTHER READING

Arnold, Nick. *Volcano, Earthquake, and Hurricane*. Chatham, NJ: Raintree Steck-Vaughn Publishers, 1997.

Griffey, Harriet. *Eyewitness Readers: Volcanoes and Other Natural Disasters*. New York: DK Publishing, 1998.

Lampton, Christopher F. *Volcano*. Brookfield, CT: Millbrook Press, 1991.

Thomas, Margaret. *Volcano!* Parsippany, NJ: Silver Burdett Press, 1991.

Van Rose, Susanna. *Volcano & Earthquake*. New York: Alfred A. Knopf Books for Young Readers, 1992.

Vrbova, Zuza. *Volcanoes and Earthquakes*. Mahwah, NJ: Troll Communications, 1990.

RESOURCES

Earthforce
http://sln.fi.edu/earth/earth.html
A site on volcanoes and earthquakes, with reports on recent disasters and disaster relief, brought to you by the Science Learning Network.

The Volcano Page
www.oink.demon.co.uk/topics/volcano.htm
This site contains interesting facts, historical information, and a glossary of volcano terms.

Volcano!
www.germantown.k12.il.us/html/volcanoes1.html
This site explains the different types of volcanoes and explains why each occurs. It also contains links to other volcano sites.

Volcano World
http://volcano.und.nodak.edu/vwdocs/movies/movie.html
This site contains a variety of video clips to view. See volcanoes erupt from a safe distance!

INDEX

INDEX

ABOUT THE AUTHOR

Luke Thompson was born in Delaware. He holds a degree in English literature from James Madison University. He lives in Vail, Colorado.